When hearts are trumps

Thomas Winthrop Hall

Contents

Kings & Queens & Bowers 7
The Perfect Face 7
The Moonlight Sonata 8
The Kiss 8
The Bride 9
A Problem 9
To Phyllis Reading a Letter 10
A Rose from her hair 11
When I told her my Love 11
My Lady, you Blushed 12
The American Slave 12
Sell Her,--That's Right 13
Time and Place 14
Blood on the Rose 15
In Old Madrid 15
The Duel 16
The Shroud 16
Love's Return 17
One Wish 17
For Me 18
To a Water-color 19
The Serenade 19
To the Rose in her hair 20
Her Reverie 21
To Beauty 22
Dreaming of You 22
Please Return 23
Almost Dying of Ennui 24
Jacks from Jack 24
Hyacinths 25
AN ECHO FROM A SEASIDE HOP 26
She Is Mine 26
Old Times 28
Of My Love 28
The Farewell 29
The Last Dance 30
Why he asked for a Vacation 32
The Editor's Valentine 33
Acting 34
An Apache Love-Song 35
The Old-fashioned Girl 36
A Retrospect 37
Hard Hit 38
Rejected 39

Jokers 39
Her Yachting Cap 39
Theft 40
Before her Mirror 41
At Old Point Comfort 42
A Drop Too Much 43
Ingratitude 43
A Few Resolutions 44
A Dilemma 45
A Choice not Necessary 45
That Boston Girl 46
The Hero 46
The Sweet Summer Girl 47
Her Fan 48
Certainty 48
Caught 49
An Important Distinction 49
Two Kinds 50
What it Is 51
In her Pew 51
The Suspicious Lover to the Star 52
A Slight Surprise 52
Past vs. Present 53

The Usual Way.	53
A Difference in Style.	54
Afraid.	55
Ye Retort Exasperating.	55
A Rhyming Reverie.	56
A Sure Winner.	57
Tantalization.	57
His Usual Fate.	58
On Two Letters from Her.	59
A Serenade--en Deux Langues.	59
When a Girl says "No."	60
Uncertainty.	61
Her Peculiarities.	61
The Reply of the Observant Youth.	62
Tying the Strings of her Shoe.	62
When You are Rejected.	63
A Bachelor's Views.	63
My Cigarette.	64
The Ice in the Punch.	66
The Tale of a Broken Heart.	67
Where did you get it?	68
No.	69
A Midsummer Night's Tempest.	70
The Abused Gallant.	72
After the Ball.	73
Vanity Fair.	74
For the Long Voyage.	75
This is the end.	75

WHEN HEARTS ARE TRUMPS

BY

Thomas Winthrop Hall

Kings & Queens & Bowers

The Perfect Face.

The Graces, on a summer day,
Grew serious for a moment; yea,
They thought in rivalry to trace
The outline of a perfect face.

Each used a rosebud for a brush,
And, while it glowed with sunset's blush,
Each painted on the evening sky,
And each a star used for the eye.

They finished. Each a curtaining cloud
Drew back, and each exclaimed aloud:
"Behold, we three have drawn the same,
From the same model!" Ah, her name?

I know. I saw the pictures grow.
I saw them falter, fade, and go.
I know the model. Oft she lures
My heart. The face, my sweet, was yours.

The Moonlight Sonata.

The notes still float upon the air,
   Just as they did that night.
I see the old piano there,--
   Oh, that again I might!

Her young voice haunts my eager ear;
   Her hair in the candle-light
Still seems an aureole,--a tear
   Is my spectroscope to-night.

I hear her trembling tell me "No,"
   And I know that she answered right
But I throw a kiss to the stars, and though
   She be wed she will dream to-night.

The Kiss

Over the green fields, over the snow,
Something I send thee, something I throw.
No one can guess it; no one can know.

Light as a feather, quick as the eye;
Thin as a sunbeam, deep as the sky;
Worthless, but something a queen could not buy.

Ah, you have caught it, love! How do I know?
Sweet, there are secrets lost ages ago.
Lovers learn all of them. Smile not,--'tis so.

The Bride.

Before her mirror, robed in spotless white,
  She stands and, wondering, looks at her own face,
  Amazed at its new loveliness and grace.
Smiling and blushing at the pretty sight,
So fraught is she with innocent delight,
  She feels the tender thrill of his embrace
  Crushing her lilies into flowery lace;
Then sighs and starts, even as though from fright.

Then fleets before her eyes the happy past;
  She turns from it with petulant disdain,
  And tries to read the future,--but in vain.
Blank are its pages from the first to last.
She hears faint music, smiles, and leaves the room
Just as one rosebud more bursts into bloom.

A Problem.

Give you a problem for your midnight toil,--
  One you can study till your hair is white

   And never solve and never guess aright,
Although you burn to dregs your midnight oil?
O Sage, I give one that will make you moil.
   Just take one weakling little woman's heart.
   Prepare your patience, furbish up your art.
How now? Did I not see you then recoil?

Tell me how many times it has known pain;
   Tell me what thing will make it feel delight;
Tell me when it is modest, when 'tis vain;
   Tell me when it is wrong and when 'tis right:
But tell me this, all other things above,--
Can it feel, Sage, the thing that man calls "Love"?

To Phyllis Reading a Letter.

A smile is curving o'er her creamy cheek,
   Her bosom swells with all a lover's joy,
   When love receives a message that the coy
Young love-god made a strong and true heart speak
From far-off lands; and like a mountain-peak
   That loses in one avalanche its cloy
   Of ice and snow, so doth her breast employ
Its hidden store of blushes; and they wreak
Destruction, as they crush my aching heart,--
   Destruction, wild, relentless, and as sure
As the poor Alpine hamlet's; and no art
   Can hide my agony, no herb can cure
My wound. Her very blush says, "We must part."
   Why was it always my fate to endure?

A Rose from her hair.

She gave me a rose from her hair,
  And she hid her young heart within it.
I could hardly speak from despair,
Till she gave that rose from her hair,
And leaned out over the stair
  With a blush as she stooped to pin it.
She gave me a rose from her hair,
  And she hid her young heart within it.

When I told her my Love.

When I told her my love,
  She was maidenly shy,
And she bit at her glove.

I gave Cupid a shove;
  Yes, I begged him to try,
When I told her my love

What was she thinking of
  As she uttered that sigh
And she bit at her glove?

And pray what does it prove
  That she stopped there to sigh,
When I told her my love
And she bit at her glove?

My Lady, you Blushed.

My lady, you blushed.
  Was my love a surprise?
How quickly they hushed!

A curl of yours brushed
  All else from my eyes.
My lady, you blushed.

You say that I gushed,
  And they all heard my sighs?
How quickly they hushed!

Your roses were crushed;
  N'importe wherefores and whys.
My lady, you blushed.

The American Slave.

Come, muster your pleasantest smile, my dear,

And put on your prettiest gown.
Forget about Jack for a while, my dear,
  His lordship has just come to town.

He's come here to get him a wife, my dear,
  And you have been put up for sale
With a marvellous income for life, my dear,
  To balance your side of the scale.

His lordship is feeble and old, my dear,--
  What odds? All the sooner he'll die.
And he has a sore need of your gold, my dear:
  See the good you can do if you'll try.

And then a real lady you'll be, my dear,
  Not only by nature but name;
Mamma'll be so proud,--you can see, my dear,
  No one thinks it, as you do, a shame.

So bend your proud head. Are you faint, my dear?
  Keep the tears back, be buoyant and brave.
Keep that pose! Now a portrait we'll paint, my dear,
  To be called "The American Slave."

Sell Her,--That's Right.

Sell her,--that's right! She is young, she is fair;
There's the light of the sun in the coils of her hair.
And her soul is as white as the first flakes of snow
That are falling to-night. 'T is a bargain, a "go"

  Sell her,--that's right!

Sell her,--that's right! For a bag full of gold.
Put her down in your ledger, and label her "Sold"
She's only a beauty with somebody's name,
And the Church for a pittance will wash out the shame.
  Sell her,--that's right!

Time and Place.

Hasten on! The mad moonlight is beaming
 On the hatred and love 'twixt us two;
And it beams on the maid who is dreaming,
 And the grave made for me or for you.

Time and place,--love and life in the balance,
 Fear and hope in the glance of your eye.
Draw your blade! Forget not we are gallants
 Who can laugh at our fate as we die.

On your guard! There'll be blood on the metal
 Ere she wakes from her innocent dreams;
There's a long list of kisses to settle,
 And some love sighs and death sighs, it seems.
Bare your arm! Strike for life and the maiden!
 Take that! You are cautious, I fear
Speed the blow,--'tis with happiness laden
 For him who does not remain here

That and that! I am wounded,--it's over

Those kisses were destined for you;
But now she is yours and you love her,
  Go tell her that I loved her too

Blood on the Rose.

Is it dew on the rose?
  'T is the same that I gave him
Last night when I chose
  To warn him and save him;

That he pinned on his breast
  With a smile at his danger,
And a smile, not in jest,
  That was sweeter and stranger

Here are footprints of foes!
  Oh, my heart!--I can feel
It is blood on the rose
  And a sliver of steel.

In Old Madrid.

I strolled the streets in quest of any love,
  In old Madrid long centuries ago;
I caught the perfume of a scented glove,

I saw a sweet face in a portico.

She laughed--then paled. She leaned out; whispered, "Fly!"
  And then I felt the sting of steel, the hiss
Of curses in my ear, and knew that I
  Had forfeited my life--and lost a kiss.

The Duel.

Ten paces--one, two, three, and fire!
Two gallants have their heart's desire.

One of them dies, the other laughs;
The seconds smile, the doctor chaffs.

A woman, smiling, dreams she's wed
To--hush, to the very one that's dead.

The Shroud.

The snow came softly, silently, down
Into the streets of the dark old town;
And lo! by the wind it was swept and piled
On the sleeping form of a beggar-child.

It kissed her cheek, and it filled her hair

With crystals that looked like diamonds there;
And she dreamed that she was a fair young bride
In a pure white dress by her husband's side.

A blush crept over her pale young face,
And her thin lips smiled with a girlish grace;
But the old storm-king made his boast aloud
That his work that night was weaving a shroud.

Love's Return.

Love has come back--ah me, the joy!--
  Greater than when Love began
To wound my heart. The jocund boy!
  Love has come back a gray-haired man.

His eyes are red with tears of woe,
  His cheeks are pale, and his heart is sore;
But Love has come back at last, and, oh!
  Love will be faithful evermore.

One Wish.

My thoughts are gliding down the stream,
  Ah, faster than the river flows;
And idly in my heart I dream

Of islands where the lotus grows.

I fear not rapids, waterfall,
  Or whirlpool leading down to death,
If love but my tired heart enthrall,
  And I may sip a woman's breath.

I care not what may be my fate.
  Roll on, mad river, to the sea;
Drown all ambition, pride, and hate,--
  But leave one woman's love to me.

For Me.

I heard her song,
  Low in the night,
From out her casement steal away,
  Nor thought it wrong
  To steal a sight
Of her--and lo! she knelt to pray.

I heard her say,
  "Forgive him, Lord;
Such as he seems he cannot be."
  I turned away,
  Myself abhorred.
She prayed--and oh! she prayed for me.

To a Water-color.

Sweet Phyllis, maid of yesterday,
  Come down from out that frame,
And tell me why you looked so gay--
  Likewise your other name.

Had bold Sir Plume confessed his love
  And asked you if you'd wed?
And had he called you "Lovey-dove"?
  And how long are you dead?

Where did you get that wondrous gown,
  Those patches, and that hair?
And how were things in London town
  The last time you were there?

And did you die a maid or wife,
  Your husband lord or knave?
And how did you like this jolly life?
  And how do you like the grave?

The Serenade.

Under my casement, as I pray,
My lover sings my cares away
With many a half-forgotten lay.

He leans against the linden-tree,
And sings old songs of Arcady
That he knows well are loved by me.

Half through the night the sweet strains float
Like wind-blown rose-leaves, note by note,
Over the great wall and the moat,

Up to my window, till they teem
Into my soul, and almost seem
To be there even when I dream.

And his heart trembling beats with bliss
If I but throw him one small kiss
Just as I now throw this, and this

To the Rose in her hair.

Poor little rose, I pity you--
  Sweet as Oporto's wind when fruity--
Tortured an evil hour or two,
  Just to adorn a wilful beauty.

I know her well, too well, alas!
  (Just watch the fairy as she dances.)
She wears my heart--but let that pass;
  It's dead: she killed it with her glances.

Your fate, poor rose, is such as mine,--
  To be despised when you are faded;

Yet she's an angel--too divine
  To be by you or me upbraided.

Her Reverie.

A lady combed her silken hair.
None but a looking-glass would dare
  To gaze on such a scene.
The blushes thronged her dimpled cheek;
They coursed upon her shoulders, eke,
  And the white neck between.

And she was thinking then, I trow,
Of one who, in a whispered vow
  Beneath the budding elm,
Had told her they would sail their barque
On lakes where pale stars pierced the dark,
  With Cupid at the helm.

Anon, a faint smile pursed her lips
And shook her dainty finger-tips,
  As breezes shake the boughs;
And then a quick, impetuous frown
Came gathering from her ringlets down,
  And perched upon her brows.

Ah, she was thinking then, I ween,
Of me, poor clumsy dunce, who e'en
  Had torn her silken dress.
I waltzed too near her at the ball;

Her beauty dazed me--that was all;
  I felt a dizziness.

To Beauty.

"Oh, Mistress Beauty," said my sigh,
  "I'd laugh to scorn all other blisses,
If you and I might live and die
  Together on such fare as kisses.

"Your kirtle would not be of silk,
  The band around it but torn leather.
I think our wine would be plain milk;
  I think we'd oft see stormy weather.

"But, oh, there are some things in life
  Worth more to men than fame or money;
And one of them's a sweet young wife,
  So pure, so honest, and so bonnie."

Dreaming of You.

My soul feels refreshed, like a rose kissed by dew,
When waking I know I've been dreaming of you.

They thought I was mad. Ah, my sweet, if they knew

That my malady simply was dreaming of you!

I've one wish. 'Tis to sleep all the long ages through
By your side, you my bride, and I dreaming of you.

Please Return.

Now, all you pretty maids in town,
  Take heed of my sad plight.
I've lost a kiss; I'll give a crown
  To get it back to-night.

I threw it, poet-like, I own,
  Up to a silvery star;
I must confess I might have known
  I could not throw so far.

But, oh, surprise! It circled round,
  And sank as though 't were laden
With love--when almost to the ground
  'T was caught by some young maiden.

And that young maid I wish to find.
  I've lost a kiss, alack!
It is not hers. She'll not be kind
  Unless she give it back.

Almost Dying of Ennui.

What are the charms of the sea?
  Oh for an hour of the city!
What are the dull waves to me?
  Can they say anything witty?

What do they care for my lips?
  Why did I come? It's a pity!
Nothing but water and ships,
  And Jack far away in the city.

Oh for one ride in the park,
  With Jack humming bars from a ditty;
Kissing me (when it grows dark).
  Fy! Oh--heigho, for the city!

Jacks from Jack.

Fresh, fragrant, tempting, balmy, red--
  What fool would send them back?
Why do I wish that I were dead,
  With all these jacks from Jack?

Why do I bite my lips and frown,
  Tear buttons off my sacque,
When, just returning to the town,
  I get these jacks from Jack?

Alas, for pleasure's giddy whirl,
  For summer lost, alack!
He's off to see some other girl;
  That's why mere jacks from Jack.

Hyacinths.

Hyacinths, tenderly sweet,
  Is it life that you ask in your prayer?
Ah, I would die at her feet,
  If I could be one of you there.

There on her billowy breast,
  So near to her innocent heart,
That its beating would lull me to rest,
  And to dream I should never depart.

Sighing are you for the stars?
  Look in the depths of her eyes.
Is there a gem of the Czar's
  So much like those gems of the skies?

Is it the dew that you miss?
  Hyacinths, hyacinths, wait.
Soon she will give you a kiss.
  Oh, how I envy your fate!

In The Waltz.

AN ECHO FROM A SEASIDE HOP.

Light as the waves foaming white on the bar,
We dance to the mandolin, harp, and guitar;
One, two, three, waltzing we glide round the room,--
Would you were bride, and ah, would I were groom!

On all the seashore none fairer than you;
What but adore you could any one do?
Cheeks like the pink of an evening sky,
Eyes that might bid a man laughingly die.

Ears like the shells from the Indian sea,
Teeth like white buds on a young apple-tree,
Throat like a lily bent heavy with dew,
Arms just as white and as lily-like too.

Lips that would tempt--ah! you'll pardon me now,
Being so near them suggests, you'll allow,
That the happiest thing e'er a mortal could do,
Would be to be ever thus waltzing with you.

She Is Mine.

There's a sparkle in her eye

That no millionnaire can buy.
If they think so, let them try--
    She's divine.

There's a blush upon her cheek
Like the peach-tree's blossom, eke,
Like red willows by the creek,
    Or like wine.

She has roses in her hair.
It was I who put them there.
Really, did I ever dare--
    Is she mine?

Or is it all a dream,--
Idle poet's empty theme
Put in words that make it seem
    Superfine?

No; for see upon her hand
There's a little golden band,--
Filigree work, understand,
    Like a vine;

And a perfect solitaire
Fits upon it. The affair
Cost two hundred. I don't care!
    She is mine.

Old Times.

Ah, good old times of belles and beaux,
Of powdered wigs and wondrous hose,
Of stately airs and careful grace,
Look you at our degenerate race.

No more the gallant spends his time
In writing of his love in rhyme;
No more he lives unconscious of
All earthly things save war and love.

We modern men have toils and cares
To streak our pates with whitened hairs,
And have to crowd our love and all
Into one short and weekly call.

Of My Love.

   Was ever a moon
   In joyous June
As royal, radiant, rare as she,
   With her smiling lips,
   As she lightly trips
Down through the autumn woods to me?

   Never a queen
   On her throne, I ween,

Had such a loyal slave as I.
   Ready to bear
   All her cares, I swear,
Just for a fleeting kiss on the sly.

   Oh for the day
   We gallop away
To the curate's cottage, Gretna Green;
   Side by side,
   Groom and bride,
Happy twenty and sweet sixteen!

The Farewell.

Not going abroad? What, to-morrow,
  And to stay, goodness knows for how long?
Really, Jack, 'twould appear that dry sorrow
  Had done even you, sir, a wrong.

It has? Ha, ha, ha! What a joke, sir!
  Is it Mabel or Jenny or Nell?
I'm sure you are wrong,--hold my cloak, sir,--
  Am I not an old friend? Come now, tell.

The prince of our set broken-hearted!
  What a joke! Who rejected you? Speak!
Did you look like that, Jack, when you parted?
  Was that pallor of death on your cheek?

You interest me. Tell me about it;

And let your old chum, sir, console.
Hard hit in the heart. I don't doubt it;
  You were made for that sort of a role.

Did you bend on your knee, like an actor,
  Hardly knowing just where to begin?
Was dear mamma's consent the main factor?
  What a fool the poor girl must have been!

Who was she? What!--I?--You were jealous?
  O, Jack, who'd have thought such a thing?
You've been certainly not over-zealous.
  But kiss me--and where is the ring?

The Last Dance.

AN INCIDENT IN A WINDOW SEAT.

He: Well, how many conquests? I fancy a score
By the flush on your cheeks and your shoulders.

She: A bore!

He: Oh, nonsense; a debutante just out of school
Who can rule with a smile what a king could not rule,
From young Harry, her prince, to myself, her poor fool!
Come, tell me, did Harry propose?

She: What a goose

You would think me to tell you, and then of what use
Could it be?

He: Well, it might give me hope, where before
There was none,--quite a boon from the lips you adore
When you 're hungry for love.

She (coquetting): Or who knows but it might--

He: Yes, it might blot from life every semblance of light
As the clouds blot the moon on a storm-troubled night.
But tell me.

She: He did.

He: And your answer was?

She: No.

He: You mean it, or are you coquetting yet?

She: Oh!
I just told him I cared for another--he smiled.
It was merely to him so much pleasure beguiled
From a girl. Charge it up profit?--loss?--tell me which?
He thinks I am pretty, they say, but, not rich.
He would love me, perhaps, for a season or two,
So I told him that I loved another.

He: And who?

She (archly): Really, must I tell *you?*

He: No--your finger--yes, this!
A solitaire--done! and now quickly!

She (feigning reluctance):   One!

He (ecstatically):   Kiss.

Why he asked for a Vacation.

"Dear Jack:
  It's delightfully gay here,--
  Old Paris seemed never so fine,--
And mamma says we're going to stay here,
  And papa--well, papa sips his wine
And says nothing. You know him of old, dear.
  He's only too happy to rest,--
After making three millions in gold, dear.
  He's played out, it must be confessed,--
And I--I'm to wed an old Baron
  Three weeks from to-day, in great style
(He's as homely and gaunt as old Charon,
  And they say that his past has been vile);
And I've promised to cut you hereafter,--
  Small chance, though, we ever shall meet,--
So let's turn our old love into laughter,
  And face the thing through. Shall we, sweet?
Can you give me up, Jack, to this ***roue***,
  Just because we may always be poor?

There's still enough time, dear, ***et tu es***
  Un brave,--you will come, I am sure.
Put your trunk on the swiftest Cunarder,
  And don't give me up, Jack, for--well,
There are things in this world that are harder
  Than poverty. Come to me!

        NELL."

The Editor's Valentine.

The editor sat in his old arm-chair
(Half his work undone he was well aware),
While the flickering light in the dingy room
Made the usual newspaper office gloom.

Before him news from the North and South,
A long account of a foreign drouth,
A lot of changes in local ads,
The report of a fight between drunken cads,

And odds and ends and smoke and talk,--
A reporter drawing cartoons in chalk
On the dirty wall, while others laughed,
And one wretch whistled, and all of them chaffed.

But the editor leaned far back in his chair;
He ran his hands through his iron-gray hair,
And stole ten minutes from work to write
A valentine to his wife that night.

He thought of metre, he thought of rhyme.
'Twas a race between weary brains and time.
He tried to write as he used to when
His heart was as young as his untried pen.

He started a sonnet, but gave it up.
A rondeau failed for a rhyme to "cup."
And the old clock ticked his time away,
For the editor's mind would go astray.

He thought of the days when they were young,
And all but love to the winds was flung,
He thought of the way she used to wear
Her wayward tresses of golden hair.

He thought of the way she used to blush.
He thought of the way he used to gush.
And a smile and a tear went creeping down
The face that so long had known a frown.

And this is what the editor wrote:
No poem--merely a little note,
Simple and manly, but tender, too;
Three little words--they were, "I love you."

Acting.

Ah, my arms hold you fast! How can they be so bold
When my hands offer nothing of silver or gold?

Can it be that I see a new light in your eye?
Can it be that I heard then a womanly sigh?

Ah, I feel such delight, and such joy, such surprise,
That I hardly dare lift my own sight to your eyes

Ah, my arms hold you fast, and my lips touch your cheek,
And I'm crying, "Love, answer me; speak to me--speak!"

And the answer you give to my longing distress
Is that word, with a blush and a kiss, that word "Yes."

Ah, my arms hold you fast, and I burn with a fire
That nothing but long-waiting love can inspire.

Yet I know you mean nothing--mean nothing, because
It's mere acting. Ah me, I can hear the applause.

An Apache Love-Song[1].

  A-atana she was here.
  A-atana I was dear.
 She will never come again.

---

1 ***A-atana***, yesterday. ***Hi-you***, where. ***A-coo***, here. ***U's-tey***, come, or bring. ***U'-ga-sha***, go, or take. ***A-oo***, yes. I have no authority for the spelling of these words. I rendered them phonetically from the pronunciation of a young Apache whom I hired to teach me the language. Many Apache words have no perceptible accent. A, here, has the sound of a in father.

Chill my heart, O wind and rain.
  A-atana she was here.

  Hark, the wind asks "Hi-you?"
    And I answer "A-coo,
Ustey with your bitter cold;
U-ga-sha, my love of old."
  Still the wind asks "Hi-you?"

"Hi-you?" I know not where.
  A-oo, I hardly care.
Take it to the land of snow;
Take it where the stars all go.
  "Hi-you?" I do not care.

  It-sau-i did it all--
  It-sau-i, proud and tall.
Tell her I have gone to fight.
Ask her if her heart is light.
  It-sau-i did it all.

The Old-fashioned Girl.

There's an old-fashioned girl in an old fashioned street,
Dressed in old-fashioned clothes from her head to her feet;
And she spends all her time in the old-fashioned way
Of caring for poor people's children all day.

She never has been to cotillon or ball,
And she knows not the styles of the Spring or the Fall;
Two hundred a year will suffice for her needs,

And an old-fashioned Bible is all that she reads.

And she has an old-fashioned heart that is true
To a fellow who died in an old coat of blue,
With its buttons all brass,--who is waiting above
For the woman who loved him with old-fashioned love.

A Retrospect.

I was poor as a beggar,--she knew it,--
  But proud as a king through it all;
Though it cost me two dollars to do it,
  I took little Meg to the ball.

Mere calico served her for satin;
  My broadcloth was made of blue jeans.
Without crest or a motto in Latin,
  Meg's style was as grand as a queen's.

And we were in dreamland all through it,
  And I do not regret it at all;
Though it cost me two dollars to do it,
  I took little Meg to the ball.

Hard Hit.

I guess that I'm done for, old chappie!
  Done, whether she loves me or not,--
But don't look so deuced unhappy,--
  Y'know it was I fired the shot.

Thanks, awfully. Give me the whiskey,--
  There's a horrible pain in my head;
It's queer that my nerves should be frisky
  When my heart is as heavy as lead.

I'm worthless; I own it! She told me,
  That night at the Country Club ball,--
Don't try, dear old fellow, to hold me,--
  Ah, Nellie!--it's over!--don't call!

She told me my life had been wasted,
  That my money had ruined my mind,
That I'd not left a pleasure untasted,--
  Had been a disgrace to mankind!

And now she's to marry another,--
  A poor man, but honest and strong,
Who had never a passion to smother,
  And never a chance to do wrong.

He loves her. They'll all think it funny
  I don't curse him and kill him, old fel;
But she loves him. I've left him my money,--
  For I love her--God bless her! Farewell!

Rejected.

Aw, yes, bah Jove. I thought you'd answer "No."
  But still a fellah 's got to awsk, you see.
And then there was the chance you might outgrow
  That way you had of making fun of me.

Three years in Europe sometimes make a change
  In girls like you, who've always been adored;
And when you laughed, I thought it rawther strange.
  Aw, I beg pawdon; p'haps you feel, aw--bored.

You don't? You think it fun--a fellah's pains
  At words like yours? You don't know how they smart.
I know you think I haven't any brains;
  But still, Miss Nellie, I've a--I've a heart.

Jokers

Her Yachting Cap.

Oh, the little yachting cap
That is lying in her lap

Has a sort of fascination for poor me.
  It is made of something white,
  And she wears it day and night,
Through the weeks she spends each summer by the sea.

  She can make of it a fan,
  And, when necessary, can
Hide her face behind it, if she chance to blush.
  It has carried caramels,
  Chocolate drops, and pretty shells,
And I've even seen her use it as a brush.

But still it has one fault
  In my eyes. I'd better halt,
Had I not, and ponder well what I shall say?
  She is darting warning glances.
  Well, under certain circumstances,
The visor's always getting in my way.

Theft.

The moonlight steals around the pine;
Star-eyes steal radiance from thine.

Low music steals upon the ear;
Can there be theft when thou art near?

I steel my heart for fear of this,--
I steel my heart and steal a kiss.

I'd steal the sacramental wine
If it were sweet as kiss of thine!

Before her Mirror.

I pause before her mirror and reflect
  (That's what the mirror does, I take it, too);
Reflect how little it has known neglect,
  And think, "O mirror, would that I were you."

She has no secrets that you do not know,
  You and yon crescent box of poudre de rose.
And even these long curling irons can show
  Much evidence of use, yet naught disclose.

Here, when she smiles, **you** know it is her teeth
  She's putting to the test ere she depart
For the gay revel on the lawn beneath,
  Or moonlight ramble that may break a heart.

Here she may blush, until she, red as wine,
  Knows that her triumphs have not ceased to be.
Here, when she frowns, and looks still more divine,
  You know, wise mirror, that she thinks of me.

At Old Point Comfort.

You don't think of dresses, or ducats, or dukes;
You don't care for chaperone's rigid rebukes;
  It's just simply grand,
  To lie there on the sand,
    Down at the beach,--
    If a man's within reach.

Some like the moonlight and some like the sun,
Some flirt in earnest and some flirt in fun;
  It's worth all the rash,
  Reckless spending of cash,
  All the dresses you spoil,
  All the tempers you roil,
    Down at the beach,--
    If a man's within reach.

It's better than sleigh-rides, cotillons, or teas,
It makes the dull Patriarch's knickerbocked knees
  Shake in the dance,
  And then one has a chance,
  If one's pretty and smart,
  With a tongue not too tart,
  Of presenting papaw
  With a new son-in-law,
    Down at the beach,--
    If a man's within reach.

A Drop Too Much.

I praised her hair, I praised her lips,
  She looked up with surprise;
I bowed to kiss her finger-tips,
  And then she dropped her eyes.

I said love ruled the world; that I
  Adored her; called her "Nan."
She merely looked a little shy,
  And then she dropped her fan.

I took the hint, and at her feet
  I knelt--yes, quite absurd;
But oh, my fond heart wildly beat
  To hear her drop a word.

I told her all: my talents few,
  My direful lack of pelf.
(We all have erred.) She said "Adieu,"
  And then dropped me myself.

Ingratitude.

Last night young Cupid lost his way,
  And came to me to find it.
He'd been a truant all the day,
  But didn't seem to mind it.

I put him in a hansom then
  For home, and feed the cabby;
But my reward was what most men
  Would call extremely shabby.

He got his bow and arrows out,
  And pierced my heart, nor tarried,
But drove away ere I could shout,
  "Great Heavens, Cupe, I'm married!"

A Few Resolutions.

(*With Reservations*)

He shall never know that I love him--
  Until he asks if I do.
And I'll feel very much above him--
  When he stoops to tie my shoe.

And I shall never kiss him--
  Until he kisses me.
And I shall never miss him--
  Till he sails over the sea.

And I shall never wed him,
  Nor call myself his bride--
Till Cupid and I have led him
  Right up to the minister's side.

A Dilemma.

A letter for me,
  From the girl that I love!
Just penned by her hand
And caressed by her glove.
  A jewel--a gem--ah!
  A letter from Emma.

A letter for me,
  Oh, what joy, what surprise!
Just kissed by her lips--
  At least, blest by her eyes.
    'T is opened--ahem, ah!
    A letter from Emma.

A letter for me,
  From my sweet little bird.
Eight pages, by Jove!
  And I can't read a word.
    A precious dilemma,
    This letter from Emma!

A Choice not Necessary.

Here is a rose,

Here is a kiss;
Which do you choose?
  One rhymes with prose;
  One rhymes with bliss.
Ah, you amuse.

  You hesitate,
  You blush, you sigh.
What! are you loath?
  'Tis getting late;
  Be quick--
Fool, take them both!

That Boston Girl.

Her voice is sweet,
  Her style is neat;
She'd move the world with but a pen.
  Her mind is clear;
  Her sight, though near,
Is long enough to capture men.
What matters it her learning, then?

The Hero.

He looked so handsome, proud, and brave,

As he stood there, straight and tall,
With his steadfast eyes, so gray, so grave,
  The beau of the Hunt Club ball.

Ah me, full many a white breast sighed
  For the favor of his hand,--
For the love of a heart so true, so tried,
  For life, you understand.

He looked a hero; he was more,
  A martyr, too, perchance;
For he went to the oldest girl on the floor,
  And led her out to dance.

The Sweet Summer Girl.

She has hair that is fluffy, straight, banged, or half curled;
Has a parasol, oft by her deft fingers twirled.
She has eyes either brown or black, gray or true blue;
Has a neat fitting glove and a still neater shoe.

She has cheeks that make bitter the envious rose;
She has trunks upon trunks of the costliest clothes;
She has jewels that shine as the stars do at night;
And she dances as Ariel dances--or might.

She knows nothing much, but she's great on the smile;
Her profession is love, and she flirts all the while;
She's accustomed to sitting on rocks in the glen;
She is also accustomed to sitting on men.

Her Fan.

A dainty thing of silk and lace,
  Of feathers, and of paint,
Held often to her laughing face
  When I assume the saint.

Too dainty far to mix with these
  Old pipes, cigars, and books
Of bachelordom,--rare life of ease,--
  Rare friends, rare wines, rare cooks.

'Twill smell of stale tobacco smoke
  Ere many days I fear,
And hear full many a rattling joke,
  And feel, perhaps, a tear.

Why is it here? Alas for me!
  I broke it at a ball.
"Apologize--repair it" See?
  Five dollars gone,--that's all.

Certainty.

Phyllis, love may be for you,

But it is not for me;
For fortune comes between us two,
  And says it must not be.

Another fellow's fortune, too;
  A million, as I know.
You ask me how I found it out?
  Your mater told me so.

Caught.

When Phyllis turned her eyes on me
  I blushed and hesitated;
For though on terms familiar, we
  Were not at all related.

I felt her mild, reproachful glance,
  And knew her words would rankle.
To tell the truth, I had, by chance,
  Been looking at her ankle.

An Important Distinction.

She said, without a single sigh,
  And hardly hesitation,
That she would be my sister, aye,

Or any fond relation.

I answered cunningly, "Ah me,
  I've sisters by the dozen;
Please make it in the next degree,
  For one may wed a cousin."

Two Kinds.

Oh, her eyes, her beautiful eyes!
How they melt when she sobs or she sighs!
  How they droop
    When she blushes!
  How they flash
    When she crushes
The love she's compelled to disguise!

Oh, her i's, her beautiful i's!
Who can tell them apart though he tries
  From her m's
    Or her e's,
  N's, or u's
    As you please
  In her letters? I offer a prize.

What it Is.

Just a little melancholy,
  Just a tear or two,
Just a word that's naughty,
  Just a spiteful "pooh!"

Just an extra cocktail,
  Just a flower-bill due,
Just another ring to take
  Unto my friend, the Jew.
That is what it is to be
  Rejected, Miss, by you.

In her Pew.

She looked up from her pew
(Why she did, Heaven knows);
But I smiled; wouldn't you?
'T was the right thing to do;
And, pshaw, nobody knew.
  Then I tried hard to pose,
  But a look of hers froze
All my blood. And I woo
Her in future, old chappie, when not in her pew.

The Suspicious Lover to the Star.

O silver star,
  That seeth far,
Tell my poor heart what she is doing;
  And ease my pain,
  Who would again
Be at her side, and still be wooing.

  Does she regret
  The token set
By me upon her slender finger?
  Or in the dance
  Do her eyes glance
At it sometimes,--and sometimes linger?

  Be, silver star,
  Particular,
And do not be afraid of hurting.
  I know her well,
  And truth to tell,
I fear my lady love is flirting.

A Slight Surprise.

Come, lovely Laura! strike the lyre,
  And I will sing a song to thee
That will thy maiden heart inspire

With love, and love alone for me.

Why hesitate? Come, strike the lyre!
  Down where the chord is minor D.
Of wooing thee I'll never tire.
  Good gracious! Why do you strike me?

Past vs. Present.

Through all the days I courted her
  My memory fondly floats,
When love and I exhorted her
  To read, re-read my notes.

But now I love her ten times more,
  And my soul fairly gloats
To think that my hard times are o'er,--
  For now she pays my notes.

The Usual Way.

Three young maidens sat in a row,
  With three grim dragons behind 'em;
And each of these maidens had a young beau,
  And they all of 'em made 'em mind 'em.

These three maidens are married now;
  In three brown-stone fronts you'll find 'em.
But ever since the very first row
  They can none of 'em make 'em mind 'em.

A Difference in Style.

Sweet Phyllis sat upon a stile,
  With love and me beside her,
Her red lips in a pouting smile.
  A pout? Her eyes belied her.

My thoughts were merry as the day,--
  And though the joke was shocking,--
I shouted quick, and turned away:
  "A spider's on your stocking!"

The fun, of course, I did not see,
  But heard an exclamation
That sounded much like "Gracious me!"
  And guessed the consternation.

Then Phyllis sat upon the style
  Of men who would deride her;
But she no longer sits the while
  With love and me beside her.

Afraid.

Down the broad stairs,
  Stranger to cares,
My love comes tripping and smiling and free;
  The snows on her breast
  Are a blush unconfessed.
I wonder what fate has in waiting for me?

  My heart seems to throb
  Like a broken-paced cob;
I fear I'm a coward in love, as they say.
  She's commencing to laugh;
  How the fellows will chaff.
By Jove, I'm not going to ask her to-day.

Ye Retort Exasperating.

"Sweete maide," ye lovesicke youthe remarked,
  "Thou'rt fickle as my star!
By far ye worste I ever sparked,
  You are! You really are!

Albeit yt my brains are nil,
  I'm gallante as can be;
I'lle be to you whate'er you wille,
  If you'lle be more to me."

"Faire youthe," ye maide replied, "I do
  Not barter, as a rule,
But I'lle be sister untoe you,--
  Be you my Aprille foole."

A Rhyming Reverie.

It was a dainty lady's glove;
A souvenir to rhyme with love.

It was the memory of a kiss,
So called to make it rhyme with bliss.

There was a month at Mt. Desert,
Synonymous and rhymes with flirt.

A pretty girl and lots of style,
Which rhymes with happy for a while.

There came a rival old and bold,
To make him rhyme with gold and sold.

A broken heart there had to be.
Alas, the rhyme just fitted me.

A Sure Winner.

Oh, treat me not with cold disdain,
  My pretty maids of fashion;
Look upon the hearts you've slain,
  And listen to my passion.

Though I am not so peerly proud
  As men of higher station,
So handsome that the madding crowd
  Collects in admiration;

And have, perhaps, too great a store
  Of sandy hair and freckles,
I've mortgages and bonds galore,
  And muchly many shekels.

You yet may journey league or mile
  To wed, as you're aware.
Come, cease your longing for mere style,
  And take   A. MILLIONNAIRE.

Tantalization.

She stands beneath the mistletoe
  As though she did not know it.
She looks quite unconcerned, you know,
  And pretty, yes,--but, blow it,

I have to turn and walk away;
  I'll have revenge anon.
She knows quite well, alack the day,
  That my wife is looking on.

His Usual Fate.

All one season
  Lost to reason,
Breathing sea air
By the beach, where
  Young hearts mingle,
Love was playful
All the day full.
  We were single.

Now with mournful
Looks and scornful
Turns he too us;
He is through us,
  Worried, harried.
Love is sighing;
Love is dying.
  We are married.

On Two Letters from Her.

I wrote her a letter. It took her quite two
  To answer it after she'd read it.
My letter contained what perhaps even you
  Have written,--at least, you have said it.

My letter contained the old tale of a heart
  That longed to be linked to another;
And I told her to think on each separate part,
  And ask the advice of her mother.

She apparently did, for the very next mail
  Brought me a message of woe.
It took her two letters; they made me turn pale;
  For they were the letters "N" "O".

A Serenade--en Deux Langues.

Sous le maple, mort de night,
  Avec le lune beams shining through,
Ecoutez-moi, mon hapless plight.
  Je vous aime--qui lovez-vous?

Je plink les strings de mon guitar.
  Il fait bien froid; J'am nervous, too.
Dites-moi, dites-moi ce que vous are?
  Je vous aime; qui lovez-vous?

Tu es si belle, je veux vous wed.
   Mon pere est riche--comme riche est you?
Bonne nuit, adieu; J'ai cold in head.
   Je vous aime--qui lovez-vous.

When a Girl says "No."

When a girl says "Yes,"
  There's a quick caress,
  A kiss, a sigh,
  A melting eye.
  There's a vision of things
  That hard cash brings,--
  A winter at Nice
  With a servant apiece,
  A long yachting cruise,
  Name in "personal news,"
  Plenty of wine,
  Two hours to dine;
But it's different quite when a girl says "No."

When a girl says "No,"
  It's so different, oh!
  No kiss, ten sighs,
  Two tear-dimmed eyes.
  There's a vision of things
  That poverty brings,--
  A winter complete
  On Uneasy Street,

A temptation to rob,
A twelve-dollar job,
A boarding-house meal,
And you pray a new deal;
For it's different quite when a girl says "No."

Uncertainty.

Jenny has a laughing eye,
Yet she is most wondrous shy.
      But why?

Jenny says she hates the men;
Still she'll marry. Artful Jen!
      But when?

I've a rival who is rich;
With one of us sweet Jen will hitch.
      But which?

Her Peculiarities.

The Question of the Learned Man.

How doth the little blushing maid
  Employ each shining hour?

Doth she, in sober thought arrayed,
  Learn knowledge that is power?

Say, doth she mend her father's socks,
  And cook his evening meal?
And doth she make her own sweet frocks
  With adolescent zeal?

The Reply of the Observant Youth.

Not much; not much. She knows it all;
  She doth not need to learn.
She thinks of naught but rout or ball,
  And which youth will be her'n.

She hustles for a diamond ring;
  She cares not for her dad.
She does not make him anything,--
  Except, she makes him mad.

Tying the Strings of her Shoe.

Tying the strings of her shoe,
  With only the moon to see me.
Could I be quick? Could you?
That is the time to woo

What would any one do?
  I tied no knot that would free me,
Tying the strings of her shoe,
  With only the moon to see me.

When You are Rejected.

Don't say
  "Good day,"
Then grab the door and slam it.
  Be quite
  Polite;
Go out, and then say, "---- it."

A Bachelor's Views.

  A pipe, a book,
  A cosy nook,
A fire,--at least its embers;
  A dog, a glass;--
  'T is thus we pass
Such hours as one remembers.

  Who'd wish to wed?
  Poor Cupid's dead
These thousand years, I wager.

    The modern maid
    Is but a jade,
Not worth the time to cage her.

    In silken gown
    To "take" the town
Her first and last ambition.
    What good is she
    To you or me
Who have but a "position"?

So let us drink
  To her,--but think
Of him who has to keep her;
  And *sans* a wife
  Let's spend our life
In bachelordom,--it's cheaper.

My Cigarette.

Ma pauvre petite,
My little sweet,
  Why do you cry?
Why this small tear,
So pure and clear,
  In each blue eye?

'My cigarette--
I'm smoking yet?'
  (I'll be discreet.)

I toss it, see,
Away from me
  Into the street.

You see I do
All things for you.
  Come, let us sup.
(But oh, what joy
To be that boy
  Who picked it up.)

Discovered.

AN EPISODE ON BEACON HILL.

You are frowning;
  I don't wonder.
Reading Browning;
  Hard as thunder!

Oh, excuse me;
  You adore it?
You amuse me;
  I abhor it.

Let me see it.
  Who has taught you?
Now to me it--
  Ah, I've caught you.

It *must* be hard so
  (Hence the frown?)
To read the bard so--
  Upside down.

The Ice in the Punch.

The wail of the 'cello is soft, sweet, and low;
There are strains of romance in the thrumming banjo.
The violin's note--feel it float in your ear;
And the harp makes one fancy that angels are near.

The voice of a young girl can reach to the heart;
The song of the baritone--well, it is art.
The flute and the lute in gavotte--the guitar
In soft serenade--how entrancing they are!
  But to all the mad millions
  Who dance at cotillons
There's naught like the clink and the clank and the crunch
  Of the ice in the punch.

So here's to the recipe, ancient in Spain,
And here's to the basket of cobwebbed champagne.
Again to the genius who grows the sharp spice,
But ten times to King Winter who furnishes ice;
  For to all the mad millions
  Who dance at cotillons
There's naught like the clink and the clank and the crunch
  Of the ice in the punch.

The Tale of a Broken Heart.

She was a
  Beautiful,
  Dutiful,
   Grand,
And rollicking queen of Bohemia,
  With a cheek that was
   Rosier,
   Cosier,
    And
As soft as a lily, and creamier.

  She was always com-
   pelling me,
   Selling me,
    I
Was her slave, but she treated me shamefully.
  She went on the
   Stage, was a
   Rage, as a--
    Why--
As a page, and they spoke of her blamefully.
  And then in the
   Papers her
   Capers were
    Writ.

I love her no longer,--I swear it;
  But I oft spend a

Dollar and
  Holler and
    Sit
Through her antics. Oh, how can I bear it?

Where did you get it?

Pray, ladies, ye of wondrous clothes,
That draw admiring "ahs!" and "ohs!"
  And "By Joves!" as men chat,
Permit me,--love the right bestows,--
  Where did you get that hat?

The very hat, sweet maids, I mean,
So often now on Broadway seen,
  That is so very flat;
Black as a rule, but sometimes green.
  Where did you get that hat?

In shape an oyster-dish,--the crown,--
A ribbon bristles up and down,
  Quite striking--yes, all that;
The sweetest, neatest thing in town!
  Where *did* you get that hat?

No

"No!" The word
Fell upon my ears
Like the knell of a funeral bell.
I had fondly expected
A whispered "yes" that
Would steal into my soul
Like the song of an angel
From some distant Aidenn.
I arose and brushed off
The knees of my trousers.
"Farewell," I said; "you have ruined my life."
"Nonsense," she replied in the cold, cutting voice
Of a woman who has been used to $100 bills
And a coupe;

"There have been thirty-seven before you, and they
Are all married and happy now.
You see I know all about young men."
"I do not think a young, timid girl
Should 'No' so much," I answered. And going out
(Carefully escorted by the butler, for there was
A better overcoat than mine in the hall),
I left her alone and unloved,--with no one to care for her
Save a couple of dozen servants
And a doting father and mother.

A Midsummer Night's Tempest.

AN EPILOGUE TO HAMLET, PERFORMED BY AMATEURS.

SCENE: Elsinore--a platform before the castle (on an improvised stage). Inky darkness. Shade of Hamlet (solus).

Shade of Hamlet: Oh, did you see him, did you see the knave,
The spindle-shanked, low-browed, and cock-eyed
Clerk to an attorney, play at Hamlet,
Dream-souled Hamlet, wearing an eyeglass?
Oh, it was horrible.

(*Enter Shade of Laertes*.)

Shade of Laertes: What's the matter with Hamlet?

S. of H.: He's not all right.
No, by the fame of Shakespeare, he's all wrong.
A certain convocation of talented amateurs
Are e'en at him.
Your amateur is your only emperor for talent;
There's not a genius in the universe
Who will essay as much.

S. of L.: Or, who will imitate nature so abominably.
Your head is level, Ham., and I--even I,
Laertes, suffered at the hands of one
Whose fiery hair, parted in the middle
Like a cranberry pie, caused me to believe
That some of nature's journeymen had made a man,

And not made him well, he imitated nature
So abominably.

S. of H.:   Ha' the fair Ophelia!

(Enter Shade of Ophelia.)

S. of O.: Yes, my lord, thine own Ophelia,
Come back to earth with heaviness o' grief
Thy madness ne'er begot, for I have seen
The efforts of a lisping, smirking maid,
As graceful as a bean-pole, and as lean.
Attempt to paint the sorrow of my heart.
Oh, I would get me to a nunnery.

S of H.:   Let me Ophelyour pulse.
Mad--quite mad; and all because
A creature whom these mortals call a Miss,
Quite properly, as her efforts are amiss,
Would fain portray thee. Soft you, now!
O fair Ophelia. Nymph in thine orisons
   Be all her sins remembered.
Why let the stricken deer go weep,
   The untrained amateur play?
All those that watch must surely weep.
   So wise men stay away.

(Flickering blue lights and curtain.)

The Abused Gallant.

Two lovely maidens (woe is me!)
  Play tennis with my heart;
And each is wondrous fair to see,
  And each is wondrous smart.

In learning, money, beauty, birth,
  None can surpass them--none.
But each receives my "court" with mirth,
  And tells the other one.

My "court"! The term is fitly used--
  A tennis court, you see.
And I know well I am abused,
  By the "racket" they give me.

Maud strikes my heart a brutal blow,
  And Mabel cries out, "Fault!"
And back and forth I undergo
  A feminine assault.

Maud asks my age. Alas! I hear
  Sweet Mabel say, "The goose
Is very nearly forty, dear."
  Maud answers, "Oh, 'the deuce'!"

And so my poor heart with their wit
  Is volleyed oft and oft,
Till Mabel cries, while holding it,
  "This heart is far too soft."

And firing it into the net,
  She says, with girlish vim,
"Although he isn't in our 'set,'
  We're making 'game' of him."

And making game they are, I swear
  By all the saints above,
With all the terms of tennis there
  Save but the sweetest, "love."

After the Ball.

A last word in the vestibule,
  A touch of taper fingers,
A scent of roses, sweet and cool,
  When she has gone still lingers.

He pauses at the carriage door
  To sigh a bit and ponder
He thinks the matter o'er and o'er,
  And all his senses wander.

With mantle thrown aside in haste,
  Her heart a bit uncertain,
And neither time nor love to waste,
  She watches through the curtain.

And she has played him well, he knows
  Nor has he dared to stop her.
She wonders when he will propose;

He wonders how he'll drop her.

Vanity Fair.

  Oh, whence, oh, where
    Is Vanity Fair?
I want to be seen with the somebodies there.
I've money and beauty and college-bred brains;
Though my 'scutcheon's not spotless, who'll mind a few stains?
To caper I wish in the chorus of style,
And wed an aristocrat after a while
  So please tell me truly, and please tell me fair,
Just how many miles it's from Madison Square.

  It's here, it's there,
    Is Vanity Fair.
  It's not like a labyrinth, not like a lair.
It's North and it's South, and it's East and it's West;
You can see it, oh, anywhere, quite at its best.
Dame Fashion is queen, Ready Money is king,
You can join it, provided you don't know a thing.
  It's miles over here, and it's miles over there;
  And it's not seven inches from Madison Square.

For the Long Voyage.

"Were I a captain bold," I said,
  And gently clasped her hand,
"Wouldst sail with me, by fancy led,
  To every foreign strand?

"Wouldst help me furl my silver sail,
  And be my trusty crew?
Wouldst stand by in the midnight gale,
  My pilot tried and true?"

"Well, no," she answered, blushing red,
  "Such heavy work I hate.
But,"--listen what the maiden said,--
  "I would be your first mate."

This is the end.

The printing was
done by John Wilson
& Son, Cambridge
for
Fredrick A. Stokes
Company
New York
MDCCCICVIII

www.bookjungle.com *email: sales@bookjungle.com fax: 630-214-0564 mail: Book Jungle PO Box 2226 Champaign, IL 61825*

The Codes Of Hammurabi And Moses
W. W. Davies

The discovery of the Hammurabi Code is one of the greatest achievements of archaeology, and is of paramount interest, not only to the student of the Bible, but also to all those interested in ancient history...

Religion **ISBN:** *1-59462-338-4* **Pages:** 132 *MSRP $12.95* QTY

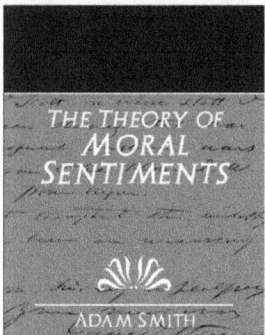

The Theory of Moral Sentiments
Adam Smith

This work from 1749. contains original theories of conscience amd moral judgment and it is the foundation for systemof morals.

Philosophy **ISBN:** *1-59462-777-0* **Pages:** 536 *MSRP $19.95* QTY

Jessica's First Prayer
Hesba Stretton

In a screened and secluded corner of one of the many railway-bridges which span the streets of London there could be seen a few years ago, from five o'clock every morning until half past eight, a tidily set-out coffee-stall, consisting of a trestle and board, upon which stood two large tin cans, with a small fire of charcoal burning under each so as to keep the coffee boiling during the early hours of the morning when the work-people were thronging into the city on their way to their daily toil...

Childrens **ISBN:** *1-59462-373-2* **Pages:** 84 *MSRP $9.95* QTY

My Life and Work
Henry Ford

Henry Ford revolutionized the world with his implementation of mass production for the Model T automobile. Gain valuable business insight into his life and work with his own auto-biography... "We have only started on our development of our country we have not as yet, with all our talk of wonderful progress, done more than scratch the surface. The progress has been wonderful enough but..."

Biographies/ **ISBN:** *1-59462-198-5* **Pages:** 300 *MSRP $21.95* QTY

www.bookjungle.com email: sales@bookjungle.com fax: 630-214-0564 mail: Book Jungle PO Box 2226 Champaign, IL 61825

The Art of Cross-Examination
Francis Wellman

QTY

I presume it is the experience of every author, after his first book is published upon an important subject, to be almost overwhelmed with a wealth of ideas and illustrations which could readily have been included in his book, and which to his own mind, at least, seem to make a second edition inevitable. Such certainly was the case with me; and when the first edition had reached its sixth impression in five months, I rejoiced to learn that it seemed to my publishers that the book had met with a sufficiently favorable reception to justify a second and considerably enlarged edition. ..

Reference   ISBN: *1-59462-647-2*   Pages:412   MSRP $19.95

On the Duty of Civil Disobedience
Henry David Thoreau

QTY

Thoreau wrote his famous essay, On the Duty of Civil Disobedience, as a protest against an unjust but popular war and the immoral but popular institution of slave-owning. He did more than write—he declined to pay his taxes, and was hauled off to gaol in consequence. Who can say how much this refusal of his hastened the end of the war and of slavery ?

Law   ISBN: *1-59462-747-9*   Pages:48   MSRP $7.45

Dream Psychology Psychoanalysis for Beginners
Sigmund Freud

QTY

Sigmund Freud, born Sigismund Schlomo Freud (May 6, 1856 - September 23, 1939), was a Jewish-Austrian neurologist and psychiatrist who co-founded the psychoanalytic school of psychology. Freud is best known for his theories of the unconscious mind, especially involving the mechanism of repression; his redefinition of sexual desire as mobile and directed towards a wide variety of objects; and his therapeutic techniques, especially his understanding of transference in the therapeutic relationship and the presumed value of dreams as sources of insight into unconscious desires.

Psychology   ISBN: *1-59462-905-6*   Pages:196   MSRP $15.45

The Miracle of Right Thought
Orison Swett Marden

QTY

Believe with all of your heart that you will do what you were made to do. When the mind has once formed the habit of holding cheerful, happy, prosperous pictures, it will not be easy to form the opposite habit. It does not matter how improbable or how far away this realization may see, or how dark the prospects may be, if we visualize them as best we can, as vividly as possible, hold tenaciously to them and vigorously struggle to attain them, they will gradually become actualized, realized in the life. But a desire, a longing without endeavor, a yearning abandoned or held indifferently will vanish without realization.

Self Help   ISBN: *1-59462-644-8*   Pages:360   MSRP $25.45

www.bookjungle.com email: sales@bookjungle.com fax: 630-214-0564 mail: Book Jungle PO Box 2226 Champaign, IL 61825

QTY

	Title	ISBN	Price
☐	**The Rosicrucian Cosmo-Conception Mystic Christianity** by *Max Heindel* *The Rosicrucian Cosmo-conception is not dogmatic, neither does it appeal to any other authority than the reason of the student. It is: not controversial, but is: sent forth in the, hope that it may help to clear...*	ISBN: 1-59462-188-8	$38.95 *New Age/Religion Pages 646*
☐	**Abandonment To Divine Providence** by *Jean-Pierre de Caussade* *"The Rev. Jean Pierre de Caussade was one of the most remarkable spiritual writers of the Society of Jesus in France in the 18th Century. His death took place at Toulouse in 1751. His works have gone through many editions and have been republished...*	ISBN: 1-59462-228-0	$25.95 *Inspirational/Religion Pages 400*
☐	**Mental Chemistry** by *Charles Haanel* *Mental Chemistry allows the change of material conditions by combining and appropriately utilizing the power of the mind. Much like applied chemistry creates something new and unique out of careful combinations of chemicals the mastery of mental chemistry...*	ISBN: 1-59462-192-6	$23.95 *New Age Pages 354*
☐	**The Letters of Robert Browning and Elizabeth Barret Barrett 1845-1846 vol II** by *Robert Browning* and *Elizabeth Barrett*	ISBN: 1-59462-193-4	$35.95 *Biographies Pages 596*
☐	**Gleanings In Genesis (volume I)** by *Arthur W. Pink* *Appropriately has Genesis been termed "the seed plot of the Bible" for in it we have, in germ form, almost all of the great doctrines which are afterwards fully developed in the books of Scripture which follow...*	ISBN: 1-59462-130-6	$27.45 *Religion/Inspirational Pages 420*
☐	**The Master Key** by *L. W. de Laurence* *In no branch of human knowledge has there been a more lively increase of the spirit of research during the past few years than in the study of Psychology, Concentration and Mental Discipline. The requests for authentic lessons in Thought Control, Mental Discipline and...*	ISBN: 1-59462-001-6	$30.95 *New Age/Business Pages 422*
☐	**The Lesser Key Of Solomon Goetia** by *L. W. de Laurence* *This translation of the first book of the "Lernegton" which is now for the first time made accessible to students of Talismanic Magic was done, after careful collation and edition, from numerous Ancient Manuscripts in Hebrew, Latin, and French...*	ISBN: 1-59462-092-X	$9.95 *New Age/Occult Pages 92*
☐	**Rubaiyat Of Omar Khayyam** by *Edward Fitzgerald* *Edward Fitzgerald, whom the world has already learned, in spite of his own efforts to remain within the shadow of anonymity, to look upon as one of the rarest poets of the century, was born at Bredfield, in Suffolk, on the 31st of March, 1809. He was the third son of John Purcell...*	ISBN:1-59462-332-5	$13.95 *Music Pages 172*
☐	**Ancient Law** by *Henry Maine* *The chief object of the following pages is to indicate some of the earliest ideas of mankind, as they are reflected in Ancient Law, and to point out the relation of those ideas to modern thought.*	ISBN: 1-59462-128-4	$29.95 *Religion/History Pages 452*
☐	**Far-Away Stories** by *William J. Locke* *"Good wine needs no bush, but a collection of mixed vintages does. And this book is just such a collection. Some of the stories I do not want to remain buried for ever in the museum files of dead magazine-numbers an author's not unpardonable vanity..."*	ISBN: 1-59462-129-2	$19.45 *Fiction Pages 272*
☐	**Life of David Crockett** by *David Crockett* *"Colonel David Crockett was one of the most remarkable men of the times in which he lived. Born in humble life, but gifted with a strong will, an indomitable courage, and unremitting perseverance...*	ISBN: 1-59462-250-7	$27.45 *Biographies/New Age Pages 424*
☐	**Lip-Reading** by *Edward Nitchie* *Edward B. Nitchie, founder of the New York School for the Hard of Hearing, now the Nitchie School of Lip-Reading, Inc, wrote "LIP-READING Principles and Practice". The development and perfecting of this meritorious work on lip-reading was an undertaking...*	ISBN: 1-59462-206-X	$25.95 *How-to Pages 400*
☐	**A Handbook of Suggestive Therapeutics, Applied Hypnotism, Psychic Science** by *Henry Munro*	ISBN: 1-59462-214-0	$24.95 *Health/New Age/Health/Self-help Pages 376*
☐	**A Doll's House: and Two Other Plays** by *Henrik Ibsen* *Henrik Ibsen created this classic when in revolutionary 1848 Rome. Introducing some striking concepts in playwriting for the realist genre, this play has been studied the world over.*	ISBN: 1-59462-112-8	$19.95 *Fiction/Classics/Plays 308*
☐	**The Light of Asia** by *sir Edwin Arnold* *In this poetic masterpiece, Edwin Arnold describes the life and teachings of Buddha. The man who was to become known as Buddha to the world was born as Prince Gautama of India but he rejected the worldly riches and abandoned the reigns of power when...*	ISBN: 1-59462-204-3	$13.95 *Religion/History/Biographies Pages 170*
☐	**The Complete Works of Guy de Maupassant** by *Guy de Maupassant* *"For days and days, nights and nights, I had dreamed of that first kiss which was to consecrate our engagement, and I knew not on what spot I should put my lips..."*	ISBN: 1-59462-157-8	$16.95 *Fiction/Classics Pages 240*
☐	**The Art of Cross-Examination** by *Francis L. Wellman* *Written by a renowned trial lawyer, Wellman imparts his experience and uses case studies to explain how to use psychology to extract desired information through questioning.*	ISBN: 1-59462-309-0	$26.95 *How-to/Science/Reference Pages 408*
☐	**Answered or Unanswered?** by *Louisa Vaughan* Miracles of Faith in China	ISBN: 1-59462-248-5	$10.95 *Religion Pages 112*
☐	**The Edinburgh Lectures on Mental Science (1909)** by *Thomas* *This book contains the substance of a course of lectures recently given by the writer in the Queen Street Hall, Edinburgh. Its purpose is to indicate the Natural Principles governing the relation between Mental Action and Material Conditions...*	ISBN: 1-59462-008-3	$11.95 *New Age/Psychology Pages 148*
☐	**Ayesha** by *H. Rider Haggard* *Verily and indeed it is the unexpected that happens! Probably if there was one person upon the earth from whom the Editor of this, and of a certain previous history, did not expect to hear again...*	ISBN: 1-59462-301-5	$24.95 *Classics Pages 380*
☐	**Ayala's Angel** by *Anthony Trollope* *The two girls were both pretty, but Lucy who was twenty-one who supposed to be simple and comparatively unattractive, whereas Ayala was credited, as her Bombwhat romantic name might show, with poetic charm and a taste for romance. Ayala when her father died was nineteen...*	ISBN: 1-59462-352-X	$29.95 *Fiction Pages 484*
☐	**The American Commonwealth** by *James Bryce* *An interpretation of American democratic political theory. It examines political mechanics and society from the perspective of Scotsman James Bryce*	ISBN: 1-59462-286-8	$34.45 *Politics Pages 572*
☐	**Stories of the Pilgrims** by *Margaret P. Pumphrey* *This book explores pilgrims religious oppression in England as well as their escape to Holland and eventual crossing to America on the Mayflower, and their early days in New England...*	ISBN: 1-59462-116-0	$17.95 *History Pages 268*

www.bookjungle.com email: sales@bookjungle.com fax: 630-214-0564 mail: Book Jungle PO Box 2226 Champaign, IL 61825

QTY

The Fasting Cure by *Sinclair Upton*　　　　ISBN: *1-59462-222-1*　**$13.95**
In the Cosmopolitan Magazine for May, 1910, and in the Contemporary Review (London) for April, 1910, I published an article dealing with my experiences in fasting. I have written a great many magazine articles, but never one which attracted so much attention...　New Age/Self Help/Health Pages 164

Hebrew Astrology by *Sepharial*　　　　ISBN: *1-59462-308-2*　**$13.45**
In these days of advanced thinking it is a matter of common observation that we have left many of the old landmarks behind and that we are now pressing forward to greater heights and to a wider horizon than that which represented the mind-content of our progenitors...　Astrology Pages 144

Thought Vibration or The Law of Attraction in the Thought World　　ISBN: *1-59462-127-6*　**$12.95**
by *William Walker Atkinson*　　　　Psychology/Religion Pages 144

Optimism by *Helen Keller*　　　　ISBN: *1-59462-108-X*　**$15.95**
Helen Keller was blind, deaf, and mute since 19 months old, yet famously learned how to overcome these handicaps, communicate with the world, and spread her lectures promoting optimism. An inspiring read for everyone...　Biographies/Inspirational Pages 84

Sara Crewe by *Frances Burnett*　　　　ISBN: *1-59462-360-0*　**$9.45**
In the first place, Miss Minchin lived in London. Her home was a large, dull, tall one, in a large, dull square, where all the houses were alike, and all the sparrows were alike, and where all the door-knockers made the same heavy sound...　Childrens/Classic Pages 88

The Autobiography of Benjamin Franklin by *Benjamin Franklin*　　ISBN: *1-59462-135-7*　**$24.95**
The Autobiography of Benjamin Franklin has probably been more extensively read than any other American historical work, and no other book of its kind has had such ups and downs of fortune. Franklin lived for many years in England, where he was agent...　Biographies/History Pages 332

Name	
Email	
Telephone	
Address	
City, State ZIP	

☐ Credit Card　　　☐ Check / Money Order

Credit Card Number	
Expiration Date	
Signature	

Please Mail to:　Book Jungle
　　　　　　　　　PO Box 2226
　　　　　　　　　Champaign, IL 61825
or Fax to:　　　630-214-0564

ORDERING INFORMATION

web: *www.bookjungle.com*
email: *sales@bookjungle.com*
fax: *630-214-0564*
mail: *Book Jungle PO Box 2226 Champaign, IL 61825*
or PayPal *to sales@bookjungle.com*

Please contact us for bulk discounts

DIRECT-ORDER TERMS

**20% Discount if You Order
Two or More Books**
Free Domestic Shipping!
Accepted: Master Card, Visa,
Discover, American Express

www.ingramcontent.com/pod-product-compliance
Lightning Source LLC
Chambersburg PA
CBHW081327040426
42453CB00013B/2321